LUNGS

AILSA HOLLAND

KU
PRESS
KINGSTON UNIVERSITY
PRESS

A catalogue of this book is available from the British Library.

ISBN 978 1 90 936288 8

Typeset in Minion Pro and Gira Sans
Photographs and Visual Work ©Ailsa Holland
Cover Design ©Jalia Pud

Editorial and Design by Kingston University Press MA Publishing
Students: Eleasah Hooper, Jalia Pud, Grace Simmonds, Caterina Somma

KINGSTON UNIVERSITY PRESS
Kingston University
Penrhyn Road
Kingston upon Thames
KT1 2EE

www.kingstonpublishing.wordpress.com
@KU_Press

There is nothing living which does not breathe,
nor anything breathing which does not live.

William Harvey
Lectures on the Whole of Anatomy (1653)

The mind and the heart follow the lungs.

Michael J. Stephen
Breath Taking (2022)

Contents

Lung

Light-headed
I peel a layer of skin,
lift scraps of iron and silk
from my tongue, from yours,
tear the pages of old books
into brittling strips, weave a
lacework of song, silences,
fingertips, flood the fabric
with blood, climb inside,
breathe again.

Living it large

I was looking for a new pair of jeans but they were all skinny and don't suit me—my husband says I have Heidi legs—even for little girls it's all skinny this skinny that, how are they meant to climb trees, I bought my daughter boys' trousers so she could move, tried to hide that from her so she wouldn't think she was the thing that was wrong, these days I mostly wear something stretchy or a dress, the kind they call maxi just to rub it in because mini would be better, you get given a number by your clothes and the smaller the number the closer you get to the front of the sexy queue and the success queue and you should always aim for zero, like Monica Rachel Buffy getting thinner and thinner, you can be cool sexy powerful witty and thin, you can't win if you're not thin, even Adele saw that eventually and doesn't she look better we were so worried about her, so don't forget to empower yourself with reading working caring for everyone and running, keep running, and always be hungry and say you're not, that green superpower smoothie is really enough till lunchtime; my daughter is so clever and she works so hard and she's mannequin thin her friends call her the Kale Queen, once after a concert a woman said to me she plays so beautifully and she has a figure to die for which made me cry in two ways; we used to sit on the sofa and watch films and eat Marmite toast, I wish she'd eat toast, the only films I want to watch these days are Melissa McCarthy dancing swearing breaking things kneeing men in the groin, am I as big as her? I'm getting bigger I guess it's the change I don't know what I'm going to change into, maybe a monster or maybe an ancient figure like the Venus of Willendorf, that would be cool, she's been curvy for 30,000 years, on bad days I curl up on the sofa in my Venus t-shirt with a cuppa watching Melissa, three goddesses living it large, extra large

Nanjizal, or, the menopausal mermaid

She sits on a cushion on a shining rock, peers
in the mussel-backed mirror, and plucks
with crab-claw tweezers the hairs that sprout
above and beneath her faded lips. Her tail
is draped to one side, but in a minute she'll
shuffle round to ease her back and her belly
will flop over the top of her scales as she bends
to read the old marks. She's very hot.

The sky and sea are big as a womb. Nanjizal
watches her daughters swim: powering, laughing
through the waves. They should be ruling
the world. It's more than half water. She smiles,
thinks of the whale-rib harpoons she's crafted
with her friends; how they're sharpened, ready.

A waste of ink

Oh, don't waste the ink
mum says as I doodle
as I let a point become a line
my name a flower, let the biro spiral
and fall off the paper, fall out of time
as I curl up in an empty dream

and the door shuts on my dream
and I feel bad for the ink
for the sad neglected time
I haven't spent properly, just doodling
so I unroll the spirals
until they're proper lines

and forget there's another kind of line
forget to build empty rooms for dreams
and if I happen to think of spirals
I wonder why and think
of ways to make sure I don't dawdle
find straight-ahead ways to spend my time

like reading reading all the time
and writing thousands of logical lines
of argument, spending my nights on oodles
of essays, making sensible marks on reams
of paper with lines on, buying ink
in cartridges (no more biro-spirals)

one night in the library I hear a spiral
—to live is so startling it leaves little time—
this joie may nought be writen with inke—
thought, to give it a proud name, had let its line
down into the stream—perchance to dream—
it seems my brain is determined to doodle

so when there are children we sit doodling
—scribbles waves clouds suns spirals—
and drink pink milk and talk about dreams
of monsters and cheese, we pass the time
walking in hops, never straight lines,
we live for paint and mud and ink

because doodling may be the best of times
and spirals are not misguided lines
and it seems my dreams are turning to ink.

Imp

One summer night she came to us, a creature
from an ancient forest, forgotten sea. She made
me scream and bleed, made me her slave. I plod
until she lets me rest, a marionette
on fraying threads; day and night she sucks
my thin white blood and drinks her fill. I thirst
for sleep, dream of running, know I'll never
be free and quite alone again. And yet
I can't but love her, find I'm happy to be
her moon. Her crown smells sweet, so new!
And outbursts of despair and rage are shortened,
stilled by the spell her face has cast on me:
her sea eyes, rose lips, her spidery black hair.
Her honey breath makes blossom out of dark.

What the buggy in the hall taught me

Time is slower than you thought. Each day
is long, exhausting and full of possibility.

Thinking isn't all that. The crunch
of a crisp packet is a happening.

Painting doesn't pass the time, it stops
and lives time, it is as essential as toast.

Glitter is not mess. Nor is mud. Every
terraced house has a step to be stepped on.

Caterpillars can be found most days, maybe
even ladybirds. Failing that, woodlice.

You can have the best conversations
with things that don't answer back.

Two-thirds of the way up the stairs
is the perfect place to read a book.

If you need to make a beach in the living-room
it will be possible. It's ok to want a t-shirt

with a goldfish on. If it doesn't exist, you
can make it. It takes as long as it takes.

Ms Euterpe

You live in close proximity to ducks
and rain and birdsong; you hear when winter melts,
when spring is greenest. Goddess-like, you bake
for soon-befriended strangers, make pea soup
for guests and sew a patchwork quilt for new
arrivals to the world: not yours, and yet.
You know that walking is a rite, and sex,
and mastering a boat through seas and locks.

Wide-eyed, you see the present bright and whole,
forget much of the past, find words in things.
Resist the lure of narrative, you say,
and know each beat of all the hours you have.
The story tells itself if you can love
and hurt and write and hear the moon on water.

What love requires... is not necessarily great busyness.

from *Advices and Queries*, 28

Once it was sitting next to you with my lunch, after you'd died, after we'd washed you, Julie and I. I loved how she talked to you all the way through, told you what she was doing, said *is it okay Joan,* and I understood that death, like birth, is women's work. It was the last thing I could do for you, make you clean. You were washed after you arrived to remove the traces of being born and we wiped away the traces of dying, we wiped the dead skin from your shoulders (later I found more underneath the sheet when I stripped the bed after they had taken you away while we hid in the living room), saw the patch where your back must've been so sore, though you said you weren't in any pain (I think by then maybe pain was the norm, pain was where you lived). Then we dressed you in fresh pyjama trousers — all the others were too big — and a nice blue longsleeved T-shirt with a print you liked, flowers, then I made a cheese sandwich and a cuppa and carried them upstairs and sat next to you, to be in the presence of your bones, to be beside the body that made and birthed me, your arms your pale hands, to have some quiet time just the two of us like when I hugged you a couple of weeks before and you said *let's stay like this forever*, the first skin to touch my skin the first person to love me. I didn't want you to be on your own. I understood for the first time why some peoples keep their ancestors' bones. I think I'd love your bones. It's at least as weird that we plan to put you in the cold hard ground, Ophelia knew, there is no doubt that women are the roots and branches, a tree will grow out of you, a leafy sister.

English fern

You
are coiled

like an easy spring,
like a wild green tongue.

Your roots are strong
and deeper than winter.

Has anything changed?
My eyes are still bluebells.

Here
is this mossy place.

What Newton didn't notice

When you sit under a tree,
the truth of gravity will hit you,
even if an apple doesn't.
Here, you are earthed.

Walk for an hour in a wood,
let yourself be pulled down
by an oak, a fir, an ash.
Feel your weight on the ground

and the world will be explained to you:
dryness by the needles between your fingers,
memory by sycamore keys,
age by roots that refuse to be invisible.

Acorns will help you understand beginnings.
Light is what works its way in.
You will recognise luck if you hear a peewit
or see a blackbird, or if

a green beetle crawls over your boot.
And maybe you will notice that moss
is its own forest and you will wish
you were small enough to enter it.

Do this for an hour, find you are still
fixed and yet floating.
You have discovered levity,
and the patchy light has found you.

Glacé

I went to the Co-op to post some poetry pamphlets — an alliterative act for an Ailsa — and shared the usual joke with the lady when she asked *is it of any value* and I said *no it's poetry*, we say that every time and laugh. We have a connection because our mums were both called Joan Holland. Mine was still alive when we found out and I was sending her something, maybe some poetry of questionable worth, and the post office lady started at the envelope and said *oh my mum's name was Joan Holland,* and since then we are weirdly mates like random women can be and we always have real conversations and she keeps one of my pamphlets by her bed to read when she retires. I'm not sure if I told her mum just died but anyway today I was sending three pamphlets and the other lady was busy and my lady quickly finished something so she could serve me, she said she likes to have too much to do, can I imagine what it's like for her colleague stuck in that little box with her three days a week and her colleague just smiled and then my lady said *yesterday, I almost killed her with a Bakewell tart.* At which her colleague smiled warmly and shyly. *Because I called out to someone* my lady said *just as she'd taken a bite and I startled her, and she choked and spat jammy crumbs out all over the glass and the office, and we laughed so much and in the evening she'd tried to tell her husband, but she was laughing* too much and then she'd told her daughter and her husband was still laughing. And now today they're back there, the two women who sit in the glass box, they keep thinking about it and laughing, and they still haven't found the cherry.

Maus

I never want to forget the time
you rang my mobile as I was
chopping veg for what passes
in our house as ratatouille,
so I put you on speaker and you told me
more amazing news —
you were having a run of it —
and I kept moving the onions
around and added the garlic
and you started to laugh
at the joke of so much happiness.

So, of course I had to laugh too,
and even though the aubergines
were sticking, there was you
on a street in the city, there was me
in the kitchen which has heard
so much chat, so much cackling, has floored
so many of our tears. On we laughed
till we couldn't draw breath, you
on the pavement, me holding on
to the worktop, until we managed to stop
and I picked up the spoon and you walked home.

Boat people

They came in a night close to Christmas,
thin and grey, with the clothes they wore
and one shoe box of things they knew.
We showed them blankets, found

it's possible to talk without words
if you smile a lot. He liked to put cake
in his soup. After half a year
he took off his hat in the house.

She wouldn't stand at the sink
to wash up. Even in a white winter
she crouched outside, her
flipflopped feet flat on the bricks,

sudding, scrubbing, the orange
plastic bowl in front of her.
We couldn't ask why and, aged six,
I knew I didn't have to know.

On my birthday they gave me
a present, wrapped in a cloth
they'd brought from home, because
the red would bring me luck.

Mr Clio

Perhaps it's strange that when I think of you
you're dressed in outdoor gear, as though for war:
a heavy khaki parka; army boots
that give a spring-skip to your step; a pair
of combats. They're camouflage, but not green
and brown for forest floor and undergrowth,
or beige and sand to blend with desert heat:
the grubby swirls are black and white and grey.
I always liked the cut and fit of them,
but only now I understand just how
perfect they are: your battleground would be
a landscape of paper mountains, fields of print,
through which you'd stride, lost, with a dodgy map,
looking for realms to colonise and conquer.

Harvest of the breathing, 2020

It started early this year. I'm old enough
to remember when tins were stacked in church,
like cold sheaves, when the leaves were turning brown,
but now we have underlying conditions.

The gleaning came first. They gathered all
our likes and loves, then everyone took scythes.
Who knew that papers dropped into boxes
could take root and sprout, could grow so big?

The reaper wears a dark suit, a careless grin.
We need to be alert. Stay home, let your children
ripen. Or shop shop shop, be part of the crop.
Your grandparents were going to die anyway.

Soon the stalk will reach the sky. Who has the axe?
When the fruit comes we'll know what we've sown.

If we're lucky, history will say this was a time of civil war

when hunger was a weapon
when being human was too pricey

when we savoured being selfish
when we cast votes to lose our freedom.

It might say this was a time

when the present became the past
when life became old films

when we became the folks in black and white
we'd always condemned.

There might be records of the times

we rose up so that when our children asked
we'd have something to say.

We shouted for Europe, democracy,
our hospitals. We didn't shout for refugees.

Someone might unearth that breath when it was clear

what was key, who we loved,
that windows should have rainbows.

To the Karl-Marx-Hof, one of the social housing blocks built by the Social-Democrat 'Red Vienna' City Council and shelled by Austro-Fascist government forces in February 1934

I

I love you because you were built as an answer to the question
what do people need to breathe?

You—and your seventy-odd siblings—said
somewhere to wash their bodies   somewhere to wash their clothes
somewhere to cook   somewhere to read   somewhere to play
somewhere to learn   somewhere to sit in the sunshine

I grieve for you because you became an answer to the question
will a government build power with the bodies of its citizens?

You came after Dachau, but before Guernica—you said
yes, there were uniforms   there were howitzers and shell-holes
there were men lined up   a woman and child lying in the snow
a police photographer   the black and white of blood on snow

I'm grateful to you because you answered the question
will there be some who resist? You said

my statues and arches and windows held firm, my people held out
as long as they could, hiding in sewers, before they were dragged
away to the Rössle, where policemen took turns to beat them,
with coffee breaks, while our leaders were hanged without trial.

II

At the century's end I sought you in the Spring, found you to be
a painted castle, saffron and ochre for blood and sunshine.
I walked through 12. Februar Platz, named in 1985,
an answer to the question *how long does it take to remember?*

To remember comrades digging up rifles, families crouched
in kitchens where the cold blasted through shellholes;
it was so cold, the air and ground were iron.
I read books, newspapers, articles, books but only understood

a year later, when I too became a space for making people.
At night I thought of a woman huddled by the stove, arms
over her children, whispering love, holding off the shells
with the arch of her back, the civilisation of her breath.

Saxon

I hid the hoard of gold to save it
for my daughters, marked the spot
with stones heaped up as if to say
'here in the earth lies a child'.

After years of battle I returned,
found the glittering grave opened,
my treasures stolen. I heard tell
they were held in a strange hall.

The house was thorned around.
To get to the gleaming I knifed
through the thickets till I sat
among my cups, torcs, swords

and dragons. Shivered. You ask
How many were hurt? How many children?
Would you have wished me wake
each day, half-dead, in a silent house?

Matter

Against all reason I like to think
there was a moment by a stream,
in the breath before dawn,

when two sat together and the air
seemed thin, missing something
they hadn't needed before,

and a single knot in a single throat
was so heavy that it shattered,
bursting from her, scattering its dust

into the cool young light
and all the people in the world
woke up that morning and found

there was green in the hawthorn
and birdsong in the oak, that
they had words for all of this

and someone to speak it to
whose face they could now
call 'beloved'.

Suitors

Most don't make a good impression at the gate;
they have limited topics of conversation,
flicky hair, no sense of humour, no good answer
to the question: What can *you* bring to the castle?

For a few over the years I've let the drawbridge down.
One had eloquent shoulders. One had well-shaped words.
One made me laugh. One was sad and completely alive.
One wore leather, but this wasn't why I liked him.

At some point I've asked most of them to leave
but I know they're all still here. When I'm working,
or walking in the garden, they pop up, uninvited,
shouting obscenities or singing a song I like.

The Mr Eratos and Mr Urania

I dreamed of E before we met: the man
who'd speak immortal words. And so I fell
heartlong for all the usual: moonlight, blooms,
talk of paradise. I'm sure he thought
he was sincere but love is deeds that come
from knowing your lover is real as you. Once free
I vowed from now I'd do the words myself.

With U it all began the day we ran
away from work to find a river and
a boat. A good man to escape with, he knew
his way around the world, would always drive
me home, saw children in the stars, amazed
me when after twenty years he said, in bed,
Don't you think it's magic, this thing called us?

It's better to have loved and lost than to be stuck with the psycho for the rest of your life

which begins now, in April, with its cruel
sweet showers, showing you what skin is for

and May, when the hawthorn blows its bright
trumpet, wears white, hides its thorns,

then June, when being outside is nicer
than your sofa, when your heart beats hot

as July, goddess of strawberries and laundry
and running from the sun you wished for

so that August is a relief because very little
happens and autumn starts to move in

and in September you buy a new notebook
because you've moved up a year

and October is proper golden for the first time
in ages and there's no dogshit in the leaves you kick

and November is damp and you want to hide
and sleep a lot and not go out in the dark

but in December you buy a tree and hang
your life on it and fill your house with green

then January comes, not as new as it promised
but this too this too will pass and all the rest

and February includes a birthday and snowdrops
who plan to raise their heads next year

and you're wise to March, one minute mild
and the next knifing, you wear woolly armour

and wait, and sure enough one day in April
the buds open, unashamed unbound unafraid

Beware of being young

Beware the daffodils the cider
because

beware the slow dance beware the headbanging
because it

beware the terrible poems, the bus shelters, the park benches
because it might
it might

beware the long walks back from the pub
beware the roll-on perfume, the pink lipstick,
discovering Shakespeare, discovering chemistry
because it might take

beware the chocolate blue of your first kiss
the black light of being hit, beware falling over
beware bleeding in exams in PE on the bus
beware the daisy chains the singing daylight
beware the whisky nighttime
it might take

beware finding the person who makes you make sense
because it might take your whole life

beware the vastness of single beds after he's gone
beware taking up smoking to kill the rest of you
beware
because it might take you
it might take your whole life to get

beware saying I love you
because it's never over

I know his name

The weaver works the frame to a frenzied beat,
a rhythm that pulses as fast as my brain,
and line by line he coaxes threads into cloth
to make you believe in paradise, or alchemy.

The fabric is for you, he shouts, as the silken colours
fly about my head, catching the light that scatters
from the many-paned windows. Nowhere holds
me in thrall like this chattering room in the sky.

Between rafter and roof I picture myself, dressed
in the raiment. Goodness, I'm lovely. I start to step
towards him, he turns. His eyes are wild. *Keep
your shiny stuff,* I say. *I'm here to get my loom back.*

Being a woman

It's about sex and solidarity. It's about
pain, periods, the perineum. It's not
about penis-envy. It's about keeping
going in spite of. It's about pockets.

A surprising amount of being a woman
revolves around cuppas: the ones we make
in each others' kitchens; the ones we drink
cold because we were needed right that minute;

the ones we hold when there's nothing to do
but feel the steam on our faces and watch
each others' tears; the ones we spill—laughing
so hard—on carpets that don't matter.

Being a woman is about the struggle of finding
a doctor who actually listens, who has
the slightest fucking clue what is wrong and what
you can do about it. Hence, it is not for cissies.

Being a woman isn't a circus of paints
and nails and lashes and heels and tucks,
it's just this body—round soft hard thin
strong hairy sweaty aching, bleeding—

which can make discoveries and art, break
records, build people, which can love like a god;
this place we all start from, the land of milk
and honey we don't remember, or ever forget.

Change

And it came to pass that Sally was on the road to Big Tescos—to get the shop in before rushing back to do the roast, phone her mum, text his mum, make sure Tom was learning his French, check Ellie had done her Physics—when a great light came upon her and she was sore afraid. Then a voice came from on high, forsooth it was a voice much like Kathy Burke's, and the voice said *Sally, Sally, they're all a load of fuckers* and lo it was as though the oestrogen-tinted spectacles fell from her eyes and she could see that she loved them and so they took her time as though it were their own, no wonder she was tired, no wonder she was hot, the rage bursting out through her skin, no wonder she would wake with aches in all her limbs. And lo she did turn the car around and drive back to her dwelling and went to bed and for three days did she stay there and did not take to herself meat or bread. Nor did she wash up or do the laundry or make lunches. And at the end of this time she named herself Paula and her conversion was complete though it took a little longer for everyone else to get used to it.

Headline

MAN, 47, found life a bit overwhelming if he'd
ever be honest, and just needed a girlfriend,

a nice girl to put him right, keep him straight.
He found one, then she found she wanted to be

a woman, not his carer, and he was devastated,
bless him, because he loved her so much;

two weeks later he was laughing in the pub
with a woman who was at a vulnerable stage

and two years later she realised she'd lost
her sense of self and gained some bruises

and moved out, he persuaded her back once
but not twice, the bitch; because then he found

true love with a woman who would never
leave him—she had old scars—and she never

did, although she tried, more than once
or twice; she was found yesterday in the park

and he sobbed, the constable said, more than
she'd ever seen anyone sob (she wondered

if anyone would ever sob that much for her
and she hoped so), he sat there next to the flat

brown suitcase with the broken zip and sobbed,
'Why do they all leave? I couldn't let her leave,

I HAD TO KILL HER BECAUSE I LOVED HER.'

Pyre

I put all the horror
in a heap, piled it high
at the edge of a cliff,

steadied myself, readied
myself to heave it over
onto sea-bashed rocks

then remembered the films
where you think the baddie
is dead and gone

but as you exhale, as your
shoulders drop, he rises again
from water/inferno/abyss.

I couldn't take that risk
so I found some fire
and set it, watched it grow

red through the black,
watched as little flakes
of charred fuckedupness

floated into the dirty air
then curled up and slept
by the embers of it.

What I want to say is

I have bled a lot, no
I laugh a lot, no
I didn't want to be a pioneer, no
There were statues, no
They all had beards, no
It got dark too early, no
I have known love, no
I have known not love, no
It began with TS Eliot, no
It began with Chaucer, no
It began with Charlotte Perkins Gilman, no
A beer can was an ashtray, no
I decided not to believe, no
I was so lost, I said no,
I was alone on an island, no
It was half a loaf, no
I have made life, no
I am less and more than, no
I have many many sisters, no
We know such things, we know

Quaker Meeting

The silence holds the air in place with hooks
hung with the sounds she hears each every week.
Dock, dock the clock makes sure that time goes by;
a page is turned, legs crossed, uncrossed, stretched out;
and there's the cough, the handbag clasp, the mints;
a stomach rolls a drum. At quarter past
the children leave, relieved of hush; without
their eyes and sighs the silence lightens, swells.

Hands clasped, eyes closed, she frowns, breathes in,
as a blackbird's song blows in with the draught.
The noises lift away, the hooks dissolve,
her heart beats loud and now she knows, as sure
as love, that there is something to be said:
it's folded on her tongue. She stands. She speaks.

Hospice at home

Jackie Sue Jen Judi Stacy Dani Georgia Kate and Angela are called nurses but what they actually do is walk alongside us, get into the boat with us, show us where to go, how to steer between worlds, how to carry on breathing, how to carry on making tea in this house where a door has opened that we didn't know was there. Every day they come into this house and love her, make all of us feel loved. If life was fair they'd be called The Women Of Ultimate Knowledge but as it is they're in their blue cotton dresses with their plastic badges and without them we'd be lost souls and with them we feel privileged, whole, rich. There are robins on the duvet cover.

You're a child again and she's just being born and you get the old slides out — of the Daf 33 and the tenements and stripy swimsuits and dad is young and mum is young — and your niece is yourself and your sister is a mother and you're all your mother's mother — the photos show some of the stuff you don't remember all the days they were there every day and the visits to relatives and holidays with needlecord flares, wellies and cagoules. Now everyone's here. A week before the end she says *I'm having a lovely time* because it's the first time in ages we've all been together, the shouting buried in being the ones who can still put the kettle on. She says to me *I love everybody* like it's a secret, a few days later she starts to go away, says her name like she's introducing herself.

She moves her hands in a different way now and we know that grief is a wisdom we won't lose and she isn't the only one preparing to go through the door, part of us will go with her and part of her will stay here because we're all one now.

The fifth day of the second month, 2023

Tonight the Staffordshire moon is full
of love, like a Stokie nurse laughing.

I breathe myself up with its cool light
so I won't be so scared when back inside

in the overwarm dark, listening to the sigh
of the mattress pump, listening

to her breathe, remembering
the long vigils with my baby son

when I willed each breath with all the force
in me, this time is different.

Diagnosis: female

It'll get better once you've had your first baby.

> (If you don't want her to miss school each month,
> we could put her on the pill.)

> You know what boys are like. Are you on the pill?

It's PMT. It's vertigo. It's in your head. I'll give you something for that.

> You can't know it's your ovary.

> Heavy bleeding is nothing to worry about.

> Are you on the pill?

> All new mums are tired.

I think that's probably in your head.

> If you're not resting I can't help you.

> Your back can't feel crunchy!

> I can't find anything wrong.

You're right at the beginning, pain-wise.

Why aren't you on the pill?

No, there's no anaesthetic. Just breathe like when
you were having your babies.

You're unlikely to get pregnant. You're worrying about
this too much.

Flu can't go on this long.

If you could do something about the weight, that would
be good.

That's not a recognised side-effect as far as I know.

It's good you've never been on the pill.

What are you really worried about?

Dr Melpomene

Tragedy is where they die at the end,
but you left halfway through Act Two.
In the lonely theatre of motherhood you played
Wise One/Witch. I brought you my despair.
You said I wasn't mad, that sleeplessness can
write catastrophic tales: fires and floods,
wars and tiny deaths. You'd played my part
in younger days; you knew this role too well.

Start now, you said, *to change the play. It's yours.*
Include some scenes where you have time to climb
a hill, pick flowers, light lamps. Write some scenes
where you sleep and some where you sweat and sing.
You had so much to give, and get, and yet.
We all die in the end. *When did you last dance?*

For Anne Hathaway, mother
of Judith Susanna Hamnet

I wish you well. I wish you the peace of evening and a way to speak to your grief if not to write it. I wish you the love of your daughters and the joy and home of women. I wish you your garden as a balm for your soul, colours and scents to fill the emptiness where your son should have been. I've read that daughters and mothers are closer, even afraid of being too alike, but a son may be the only person for whom you will ever be perfect, and your children should still be in the world while you are to help your breathing. I wish you breathing. I wish you sleep and dawn and dew on your feet to make your tears their sisters. I wish you colours. I know you will have to make your own colours. I wish you take the time you need. I wish men were more useful, less selfish, more able to see what the real work is. I wish you strawberries, apples. I wish you the spring green of hawthorn and the golden leaves of the silver birch in autumn. I wish you frost on the heads of cow parsley, patterns of stars. I wish you feel your boy with you while you work, when you go to sleep, when you close your eyes for the last time.

Ms and Mr Polyhymnia

Music is much like a garden: beloved,
backbreaking, relentless. For both
of you it was a favourite place to go. I feared
it wore you out more than it brought you joy:
the notes were too high or the rhythm was
Stravinsky; the same piece echoed through the house
so often that madness threatened to move in
and I longed for silence, my estranged old friend.

But now you've gone I carry music with me:
see you sat, string straight, head keenly slant, hands
bouncing the bow, running on the board;
or standing bright, your mouth a gate for the sound
a big heart makes. I see you in colours, so
utterly completely and more than yourselves.

Memories of my children's future

We locked ourselves in with the spring, sat
with the bees, the birds, the blossom clouds,
the hawthorn bursting into green, so green.
Outside the fire was spreading.

Inside we built a table-top treehouse. Giddy,
the two of you planned a life in the woods:
rope bridges, pulleys and a tree-top raft.
It would all be roofed by sunlight.

Plant the trees now, I want to say, *so they'll be ready.*
It's good to get away from the ground. Know that
there will be winters, that you'll sing with the nightingale.
I want to say, *Hide out in the rooms*

that float in the beech leaves, remember the sparrows
in the hedge at home, the buzzing in the clover;
remember the wren, the silver birch queen. Don't ever
give up your names, or the moon.

When I think of London I think of the British Museum

and those summers when the sky was always blue
and a Bloomsbury guest house was briefly our home
and my son and I could just pop in when the sun
was a little lower, when the place was full enough of life
but there was space to dream around the things
and the Great Hall was all light and glass and stone.

Once we met an ancient goddess, made of stone
by the Huastec people, later defeated under blue
skies by the Aztecs. We only know them by their things.
She's a mother goddess: her jobs are to keep the home
clean by eating the filth, to make new life
out of dirt. Her headdress has rays like the sun.

There was a helmet of gold that shone like the sun,
found before a war in a mound of earth, with a stone
sceptre and garnet jewels. It was worn to preserve life
when swords clashed and battle horns blew.
The dead were laid in ships when to make your home
by the sea was to live at the centre of things.

We saw for real a picture we knew from so many things
but had never really seen, made by the son
of a mirror-maker: men in boats, trying to get home.
With the first pigment not made of crushed stone
or plants or animals, it gives us a giant wave of blue.
(Dying, the artist asked for more years of painting life.)

There was a case that reminded me of my younger life
when I collected badges, among other cheap things,
at a time when it seemed that any day our little blue
planet would be blown to dust. We marched in the sun
to stop the bomb; at my high school in Stone
I wore the only CND badge, always glad to be home.

And a Lion Man! Found in pieces in the home
of people who hunted and gathered to stay alive,
made from mammoth ivory with tools of stone
by someone who made time to think of things
that don't exist, who made them real. She sat in the sun
with her children, or in the cave when the wind blew.

From all the visits to that home of salvaged things,
what will stay alive in me is the moment my son
smiled up at me in that stone hall, under a roof of blue.

Jungle Gym

ENCLOSURES
Susie Campbell

CrO[...]NG
FRI[...]
NG
àRd
SeN
eR

TROUBLED
TIMES:
Macclesfield
1790-
1870

AN ANTHOLOGY OF
SCOTTISH WOMEN
POETS
Catherine Kerrigan
EDITOR

Laura Davis

Found & Lost

KISSING
THE ROD

[...] TYRRELL

PRESENTLY

Distractions

It used to be young men who stopped me working,
keeping me from my essays with their eyes, their shirts,
that scent of savoury cloves, their clever conversation.

Then, children. *Don't read, look!* And there had to be time
for stories, drums, paint, fights, swings, biscuits,
for a warm body on a sofa teaspooned against mine.

And now my cat sits on this book, covering as much
as he can, gnashing at the pen, headbutting my hand,
purring into my chest. So I give up, give in, stroke

his belly. He claws me tight, teases with bites like kisses,
arches his back, makes a soft roar, curls into sleep.
I ask, again, *Should I write more, love less?,* pick up my pen.

Vanilla variations

There's friendly sex, full-throttle sex
tired-and-absent-minded sex
sex-because-it's-Thursday-sex

making-an-effort-to-talk-dirty sex
this-is-the-last-time-
although-he-doesn't-know-it sex

drunk-probably-a-mistake sex
tipsy-rather-successful sex
sober-and-athletic sex.

There's sex when you begin
breathless with the beauty of him
and end up underwhelmed, but also

surprised-he-knows-his-stuff sex
keeping-quiet-in-a-tent-sex
making-up-after-cruel-words-sex

and trying-to-get-pregnant sex,
when you are in the future as well
as the present and then there's

sex when a loved one has died
and both of you are crying
and this is how we are alive.

What if

What if I'd got up while it was still dark
and packed a bag to travel light
and walked to town to catch a bus

then jumped on the sleeper train?
What if meanwhile you'd got on a plane
to a place of shiny shoes and broken feet

and we planned to meet on a sunny street,
but I found a ferry I couldn't resist
and you rented a car for Route 66

and our paths might have crossed
but I got on the tram and you lost
my number on the underground

and we found though still fond
we were headed in different directions
on opposite sides of the pond.

Would it matter? Would I wish
I'd woken you, would you wish
I'd called? Is this, in fact, what we did?

Ms Calliope

You were quite often late — once it was hours —
because you'd been waylaid, you said, by flood
or earthquake, tall and handsome stranger.
We loved them all — the one about the bull
and the water jug; the one about the salmon
and dancing the conga to Mahler's Fifth.
And no-one can be cross when doubled up.
We knew there was no line between truth and tale.

No wonder then that this became your work –
the stories that scraped the sky turned to scripts
with arcs, dénouements, folk who make us laugh
and break our hearts. You see the mess we make
of things; it makes you love us more. Your eyes
are dark and light as truth and lies, and shining.

The first time it might have happened

I could have been wearing my green waistcoat and sitting in the park. There was cherry blossom like the tree we had where I used to hide and a dog walked past attached to a man wearing lots of purple with a huge moustache that twitched and he was singing; a plane flew overhead a woman in a red cloak tried to throw a newspaper in the bin it landed on top of me she was on her phone I said *hey lady* she dropped the paper on the ground, the pages separated and blew everywhere, as though someone was about to start painting, and a child rode over the paper on a tricycle round and round, giggling, with pink tassels on his handlebars; there was municipal planting and a bubbling fountain, which every few minutes burst up unexpectedly, making everyone shriek with laughter, except for one man who burst into tears and ran away, unless he was going to do that anyway; there were trees trees with blossom and trees with new leaves and a path and litter bins. The boy tricycled away and I picked up the newspaper, put it in the bin and started my dances, the dances I could do when it's spring and there are trees and I'm wearing my green waistcoat. At first, no one joined in, but then a couple of kids did and then an old lady holding a ticket from the underground, waving it above her head as though she was claiming a prize in the school raffle, like *I've got green 57* and swinging her hips left and right, anywhere she could, and holding her shopping trolley with the other hand like she was the prow of a ship, and that was her anchor, but still, she was moving, blowing in the breeze, still moving, still alive in the park with the blossom, remembering the first time she was here, and who she kissed and dancing dancing

Ms Terpsichore

At the first lesson we were shy, hoped we didn't
look daft in old leggings, big t-shirts, new shoes.
Would we be able to keep up? It was ages
since we'd gathered in a room of reflections.
We stood on one leg, wobbled, giggled. You
said we'd get stronger. We pointed and bowed,
reached and stretched. You taught our bodies
new shapes, how to write a story out of steps.

So this is dancing. This is how it felt to be alive
before the mirrors started looking back.
We can balance, we can spin, we feel the floor
through our feet, discover that the earth
is somewhere to stand tall, jump off from. We own
the world, all queens. We never ask who's fairest.

For you I would walk through fire or over hot coals

I would take bullets fired at you into the soft mass of me. I would climb a mountain carrying you to reach a necessary border I would hunger into hallucination rather than hear your empty cry. I would wrestle a tiger to give you time to run. I would give you my coat, my cardigan and my T-shirt to stop your shiver.

I will try to be what you need me to be so you can be happy in 10 20 50 years. I will walk at your pace, absorb your frights, be fearless for you. I will watch CBeebies repeats. I will wake with you when you are ill. I will listen to music you like, read a book a thousand times, sing the same songs every night.

I will take a path in the wood. I will put my ego in a drawer. I will miss it. I may forget it's there. I will give you my minutes and years. I will fight to stay conscious in the afternoons. I will take the boredom, terror and insanity because you are the best reason I ever, because why should someone else, because breathing is hard without, because there is no other contract offering utter daily joy.

Perpetuum mobile

I was three when the grandmother who loved me left me
the automaton she'd built after marriage, between laundry
and grieving her first born, between caring for my mum
and keeping her budget to the farthing.

You can still see the parts: tobacco tins, chipped plates,
stamps from her Ma's letters, a cotton tablecloth stained
beyond saving, the cogs and springs she'd kept
from the clock that stopped when she was a girl.

Each morning it hums into life by the kettle,
begins to draw a picture, the same one every day.
When it starts to wind down it sings and the springs
are taut again. In the evening, its energy almost gone,

it dances a mechanical jig to revive itself. At night
it seems to rest but it's always ticking. I could believe
it breathes. I've owned it through girlhood, student
days, motherhood, never seen the whole picture.

A German girl

Nothing is more unworthy of a cultured people than to allow itself to be governed, without resistance, by a ruling clique that is irresponsible and driven by dark ambitions.

(White Rose leaflet, June 1942)

Resistance was much on my mind that summer,
as I watched the cogs in the machines: metal, oiled,
precise, and ignorant as clocks. I had a memory of
skipping in formation in blonde sunshine. I pictured
myself with a fistful of sand to throw in the works.

In the autumn I was often awake at night, turning
a handle, churning out small papers to scatter
in the streets and squares. In the mornings I kicked
my way through the beech leaves in the English Garden.
My arms ached and the trees glowed like first love.

I spent many winter days strewing facts through
letter boxes in Freiburg, Stuttgart, Innsbruck – a slow,
cold sower. In the evenings, when my tired legs walked
back through Munich, I loved each snowflake as it fell.
I understood the ice-flowers on the window of my room.

Here in your so-called court it's clear how this will end.
*A fine, sunny day, and I have to go, but what does my death matter
if through us, thousands are awakened and stirred to action?*
Spring will come soon; horse chestnut buds will burst
into soft green. You will never rub us out of your eye.

Mary Magdalene in the desert

Listen, tossers: meeting him was a revelation.
He took my jar of oil, gave me a foot rub.
He listened to me, liked what I had to say.
God, that was a different way of being alive.

I lost him in the end as I should have known
I would, though he'd spouted all that bollocks
about coming back, about always being
there for me. He was a man, after all.

But then I happened to tell a friend
I'd seen him walking near the tomb,
and the whole bloody thing got out of hand.
I see him all the time, gobshites. Everywhere.

I came here to escape the whole friggin' circus.
Living alone in a cold dark cave
can be very appealing to a woman.
I think it's the total lack of morons.

At first I cried every night and every morning,
even though and because there was nothing
between me and the soft sunrise,
between me and the red sun leaving.

My hair grew, long as rushes; my skin got tough.
One morning I washed in a pool after rain;
anointed my hands and feet. A bird sang;
I knew two things. I held my face up to the sun.

In Macclesfield Forest

there's a tree as big as a woman
who's as big as a tree who's a woman
there's a house without a roof
and a stream with a bridge
in a place so dusk only ferns could love it,

and a sloping meadow where grass
shouldn't grow, there's grass only
on one side of the path
the other side is steep and bare
and looks a bit dry and a bit like death

but in there somewhere is the beginning
of water, you can climb down to the stream
like the woman-tree who stands by the bridge
and loves the ferns who love the dusk,
who loves the rocks—at night she climbs

up to them, hooks her arm around the cairn
curls herself around the peak in her green coat
up here she can breathe for miles, and sleep
and dream of the house that used
to have a roof, when she was small,

when she saw the meadow through the window,
shining between the trees as the grass
that shouldn't be there caught the sun
and made her smile, and because it was
too lovely to be seen through a window

she began to grow, shoved the slates
into the woods, cracked the rafters
with her crown, stood as tall as a tree
so she could see more clearly
what shouldn't be there, the gold of it

Norman MacCaig said it takes as long to write a poem as it does to smoke a cigarette (or two for a long one), but I've given up

I would love to burn again
like a match lit then turned
to let the flame rise up

how long can you hold it?
will you use your nails?

I would love to burn
like a match on a dark
inside a friend's cupped

have you got your mother's
asbestos fingers?

to burn like the first flame
in the fire you built
the fire you will love

do you remember
when bowing your head

through its bright tentative youth
its blazing ripeness
its blood red embers

to light a fag was like
leaning in for a kiss?

I would love to whistle
through damp branches
on a mountain,

do you poke the fire,
make it flare?

burn purple with driftwood
on a beach,
calling to the pull of the sea

did you think it could burn hot
and forever?

I would love to find
the roots of me blackened
like a moorland, after swaling

Miserere in the mirror, or, a non-sonnet to my body, nuddy, without a stitch or a bonnet on it

I was always dissatisfied with you:
too curvy, too hairy; with legs made
for mountain paths not mini-skirts;
with northern arms, made for
kneading bread and scrubbing steps.

I put smoke inside you, and darkness,
and I'm sure you remember that time
with the vodka. We've had to get good
at pain: surgery, childbirth, that monthly
bleeding torture. We know how to love

and be loved. We know the power
of presence, of fingertips, of breath.
Looking in this mirror framed with silver,
I see some grey amongst the black.
I see Michelangelo's Eve; one

of Nikki de Saint Phalle's bright giants;
and when I turn my back and peek
over my shoulder, there is Man Ray's cello.
You are still here, you are still upright,
you are still singing. Forgive me.

Weekend

In A & E there are people who can save your life
but not enough pillows
and the curtains around the cubicle have bruised stripes,
and a girl, high on something, or low,
is kicking a door and screaming *Give me my bag!*
but they won't because they think it has a knife in it
and her friend is effin' and jeffin'
and the police have been called
and a voice booms, again, *Can anybody hear me?*

On the Observation Ward a bag of salt water
drips patiently into my veins and I wonder
When I wake up, will I be a mermaid?
and the cubicle curtains are decorated with septic blocks
and the doctor asks questions and Irene tries to answer.
What year it is, what job she used to have.
Irene thinks she is doing quite well.
She hasn't heard of the Second World War.
What a lot of questions, she says. *Are you self-employed?*

When it's time, Rod the tired staff nurse
takes both my hands and walks with me
to the anaesthetist, who says yes,
if I think happy thoughts I will have happy dreams
and I go to a place where the ferns are green green
and the mosses are lit with water drops
and the sun rains down through the trees
like cool kisses.
I wake up, smiling.

In Surgical Assessment one of the nurses is crying
and on the curtains there are rectangles
with rounded corners, like bacteria, or old plasters,
and the lady opposite would like some water
but there are no jugs left, and in the night Mary is sick,
and the nurse sits with her and talks so gently
and Ally, who's had cancer and all sorts,
massages her sore right heel
because after two days on the same ward
they're considerably more than family.

The only proper way to go on a fossil hunt is in a minibus

She was always glad to be taken along, liked
the dirt, the students' laughter.

Once, in the pale grey slope of a road cutting,
she found an ammonite, big as a skull.

Having learned that the earth is made of layers
she began to put her feet down differently

so as not to disturb the pattern, dreamed
of shapes vibrating in the seams,

found she was torn between the wish to preserve
and a digging desire to excavate,

cover the landscape in mountains of rubble,
unearth old life or an ancient ore.

She longed for a map that could pinpoint
a likely place to look, spare her

the lung-blighting spade work. Better to lie still
with her ear in the cool grass, listen

to the coal,
to the trilobites singing.

Bones

I watched a woman who could read bones. I try to read pieces of wood I find in the forest which are tree bones and I try to read stones I pick up on the beach which are the bones of the earth. The trees and the earth are our ancestors. I think the first wand was a rib which had moved with all those breaths and sighs, which had felt the catch which didn't end which knew the paths knew the doors between the living and the dead. I stand above my mother's bones remembering. You can play music on bones because they sing of death and living on.

Once, and for all

Because I'm running out of energy and let's face it
years, I'm going to do it today once and for all
and thereby save myself, my sister, my daughter
and all the others time because of course
they're all my sisters they're all my daughters;

I'm going to just do it right here in this poem,
I'm going to create a world where it's possible
so we don't have to create a whole new world every
single time because it's a waste of power a waste
of our breath, so here goes, I'm doing it,

in this world there is a forest (and because I can,
I think I might make there be bluebells
and lots of birds) or a street (and because
it would be nice, there'll be beech trees there)
or an office (and while I'm here, I'll make it

so she's found something to wear for work
which is smart and comfortable, doesn't
make her sweat, can be bunged in the wash
and doesn't need ironing) or a school (and to save
more time, I'll make it so history lessons

are as much about women as men) or a factory
(where people get to change jobs, which is slightly
less cost-effective, but no one is dying of boredom)
or a bedroom (the definition of 'bedroom' is
'the never-feel-scared-room'). So wherever we are, here

we are. You know her or you don't. She's wearing
boots or stilettos or Clarks shoes or safety shoes
or she's barefoot. The sun is shining through the trees
or it's dark apart from the one flickering streetlight
or it's end-of-the-day stuffy or it's raining

on the corrugated roof or the curtains
are open just a crack. You make a suggestion
with a question with your eyes with your hand
or in an email or a WhatsApp message or a whisper
and she replies looking you straight in the eyes

or looking at her feet, or with a kind one-liner
and a smiley or with her hand or by stepping away,
and you're okay with that, because these are her rights:
to say this is how it is and be believed to say this
is how I feel and be respected to speak the word that isn't yes

Joan

She drew her first breath in Denton Burn, at home, cut at last
from her caul, as a girl she'd get breathless with excitement
when the Hoppings came to the Town Moor, when Grandfather
let her help in the shop on the Royal Mile. After the war she caught
her breath at the view of Bavarian lakes and mountains, later
in London a cravatted young man might have taken her breath away

She gave deep breaths in rhythm as she pushed us both out,
lots of times she should have saved her breath because we
knew better, too often she wasted her breath on Tory voters
on doorsteps and once bated her breath while waiting all night
to see if things would get better; the sigh of relief she breathed
was all-too short-lived, she roared at the betrayal.

After the op she suffered from shortness of breath, one day
she said *I want to disappear.* She wanted to take her last breath
at home, *no experts,* three days before the end she woke
in the dark, whispered *Ailsa? What's going on? Are you blowing
my face?* and I said *Yes Mama,* took her hand and pictured
where she might be, somewhere light, taking the air

Ms Thalia

Your garden is a stage set for a play,
framed by apples and silver birch, papered
with honesty, garlanded with ivy,
with places to hide and a driftwood arch
that smells of sea. In dungarees and boots
you know that happiness is made of work
and waiting, that joy is found most easily
with a backdrop of fairy lights and leaves.

Many hours we've watched the birds perform,
mugs in hands, taking turns to reenact
the dramas of the week, workshopping what
could happen next, imagining we might
not fail this time. We cry, but when a poem
is written in green that's never how it ends.

MONT
BLANC
60 ml INK

LAVENDER PURPLE

Parker

Ailifesto

poem is itself   poem is found by mining
is coal ore jewel   poem is salt   poem says
this is how it feels to wear this skin in the
world   poem is map mallet magnifying glass
poem is the broken spoken

poem is inside outside   poem is moss
poem makes scent   poem is the woods
poem walks without swagger   poem is late-
night confidences early-morning terrors
poem spells words to touch

poem says body knows   poem writes with
gold and mud   poem is clear water   dive in
find the green   poem is flashing light   poem
is lung built of bones   poem whispers *burn
after reading*   poem refuses despair

Acknowledgements

Many thanks to Steve Fowler and the Popogrou collective who were the first to see my weird lungs photos and gave me the heart to keep going.

Thank you to Emma Tait and the team from Kingston University – Eleasah Hooper, Jalia Pud, Grace Simmonds and Caterina Somma – it's been a pleasure to work with you all.

Thank you to all those friends and amigos who make breathing fun, and who check in when it's hard. You know who you are.

Thanks to Lili and Ben for making the world more wonderful.

And thanks to Robbi for saying 'but you're a poet!' and never asking why I don't do something else.

Notes

'Weekend' won second prize in the Open Category of the 2014 Hippocrates competition and was published in Michael Hulse and Donald Singer, eds., *The Hippocrates Prize* (2014).

'Mary Magdalene in the desert' won the Manchester Cathedral Poetry Prize 2019.

'Matter' was published in my pamphlet *Twenty Four Miles Up* (2017).

'Ailifesto' was hand typeset and printed in an edition of 25 on a Gem letterpress at Hot Bed Press, Salford.

These poems, or earlier versions of these poems, have been previously published in journals and anthologies:

'What Newton didn't notice' in Michael McKimm, ed., *The Tree Line: poems for trees, woods and people* (2017)

'Mr Clio' as 'Mr History' in Angle 5 (Spring/Summer 2014)

'Suitors' in *Lighthouse 20* (Autumn 2019)

'Pyre' in *The Rialto 92* (Spring 2019)

'Vanilla variations' in *Bare Fiction 11* (July 2018)

'A German girl' in *Noble Dissent: A demonstration of poetry that toes no lines* (2017)

'Miserere in the mirror, or, a non-sonnet to my body, nuddy, without a stitch or a bonnet on it' in *The Dark Horse 45* (Summer 2022)

'The only proper way to go on a fossil hunt is in a minibus' in Michael McKimm, ed., *MAP: Poems After William Smith's Geological Map of 1815* (2015)

About the author

Award-winning poet Ailsa Holland published her first collection, *The Bodleian and the Bottle Ovens*, with Kingston University Press in 2023. Her pamphlet, *Twenty Four Miles Up*, was published in 2017 with support from Arts Council England. Ailsa's poems have appeared in anthologies including *The Tree Line* (2017) and *The Very Best of 52* (2015) and in journals such as *The Rialto, The Dark Horse, Under the Radar and 3:AM*. She has collaborated with visual and sound artists on several exhibitions including *Scientific Rambles* (2025) and *How Did It Get So Dark* (2018-19); she was Artist-in-Residence for Macclesfield's Barnaby Festival in 2016. Ailsa is co-author of *On This Day She: Putting Women Back Into History, One Day At A Time* (2021). She is Director of Moormaid Press, a publisher of poetry pamphlets.

ailsaholland.co.uk
moormaidpress.co.uk

About Kingston University Press

Kingston University Press has been publishing high-quality commercial and academic titles for more than ten years.

KUP's mission is to publish voices that reflect and appeal to our community at the University as well as the wider reading community of readers and writers in the UK and beyond.

Since 2015 all the books we have published have been produced by students on the MA Publishing and BA Publishing courses, working with authors from within our academic community and collaborative partners from the wider community.

Follow us on X @KU_Press

This book was edited, designed, typeset and produced by students on the MA Publishing course at Kingston University.

To find out more about our hands-on, professionally focused and flexible MA and BA programmes please visit:

www.kingston.ac.uk
www.kingstonpublishing.wordpress.com
Follow us on Instagram @kingstonjourno

www.ingramcontent.com/pod-product-compliance
Lightning Source LLC
LaVergne TN
LVHW022325080426
835508LV00013BA/1322